Title Withdrawn

Issue #1
Spring 2008

biography for beginners

Sketches for Early Readers

Laurie Lanzen Harris,
Editor

Favorable Impressions

P.O. Box 69018
Pleasant Ridge, Michigan 48069

Laurie Lanzen Harris, *Editor and Publisher*
Dan Harris, *Vice President, Marketing*
Laurie C. Hillstrom, *Sketch Writer*
Catherine Harris, *Copy Editor*

Favorable Impressions
P.O. Box 69018, Pleasant Ridge, Michigan 48069

ISSN 1081-4973

Contents

Preface

Biography for Beginners is a publication designed for young readers ages 6 to 9. It covers the kinds of people young people want to know about — favorite authors, television and sports stars, and world figures.

Biography for Beginners is published two times a year. A one-year subscription includes two 100-page hardbound volumes, published in Spring (May) and Fall (October).

The Plan of the Work

Biography for Beginners is especially created for young readers in a format they can read, understand, and enjoy. Each hardcover issue contains approximately 10 profiles, arranged alphabetically. Each entry provides several illustrations, including photographs of the individual, book covers, illustrations from books, and action shots. Each entry is coded with a symbol that indicates the profession of the person profiled. Boldfaced headings lead readers to information on birth, growing up, school, choosing a career, work life, and home and family. Each entry concludes with an address so that students can write for further information. Web sites are included as available. The length and vocabulary used in each entry, as well as the type size, page size, illustrations, and layout, have been developed with early readers in mind.

Because an early reader's first introduction to biography often comes as part of a unit on a writer like Dr. Seuss, authors are a special focus of *Biography for Beginners*. The authors included in this issue were chosen for their appeal to readers in grades one through four.

There is a broad range of reading abilities in children ages 6 to 9. A book that would appeal to a beginning first-grade reader might not satisfy the needs of an advanced reader finishing the fourth grade. To accommodate the widest range of readers in the age group, *Biography for Beginners* is written at the mid-second grade to third grade reading level. If beginning readers find the content too difficult, the entry could be used as a "read aloud" text, or readers could use the boldfaced headings to focus on parts of a sketch.

Indexes

Each issue of *Biography for Beginners* includes a Name Index, a Subject Index covering occupations and ethnic and minority backgrounds, and a Birthday Index. These indexes cumulate with each issue. The indexes are intended to be used by the young readers themselves, with help from teachers and librarians, and are not as detailed or lengthy as the indexes in works for older children.

Our Advisors

Biography for Beginners was reviewed by an Advisory Board made up of school librarians, public librarians, and reading specialists. Their thoughtful comments and suggestions have been invaluable in developing this publication. Any errors, however, are mine alone. I would like to list the members of the Advisory Board and to thank them again for their efforts.

Linda Carpino   Detroit Public Library
                 Detroit, MI

Nina Levine   Blue Mountain Middle School
                 Cortlandt Manor, NY

Nancy Margolin   McDougle Elementary School
                 Chapel Hill, NC

Deb Rothaug   Plainview Old Bethpage Schools
                 Plainview, NY

Laurie Scott   Farmington Hills Community Library
                 Farmington Hills, MI

Joyce Siler   Westridge Elementary School
                 Kansas City, MO

Your Comments Are Welcome

Our goal is to provide accurate, accessible biographical information to early readers. Let us know how you think we're doing. Please write or call me with your comments.

We want to include the people your young readers want to know about. Send me your suggestions to the address below, or to my e-mail address. You can also post suggestions at our website, www.favimp.com. If we include someone you or a young reader suggest, we will send you a free issue, with our compliments, and we'll list your name in the issue in which your suggested profile appears.

And take a look at the next page, where we've listed those libraries and individuals who will be receiving a free copy of this issue for their suggestions.

Acknowledgments

I'd like to thank Marco Di Vita for superb design, layout, and typesetting; Catherine Harris for editorial assistance; Barry Puckett for research assistance; and Kevin Hayes for production help.

Laurie Harris
Editor, *Biography for Beginners*
P.O. Box 69018
Pleasant Ridge, MI 48069
e-mail: laurieh@favimp.com
URL: http://www.favimp.com

Congratulations

Congratulations to the following individuals and libraries, who are receiving a free copy of *Biography for Beginners,* Spring 2008, for suggesting people who appear in this issue:

Sister Jeanette Adler, Pine Ridge Elementary, Birdseye, IN

Carol Blaney, Conley Elementary, Whitman, MA

Karen Locke, McKean Elementary, McKean, PA

Photo and Illustration Credits

Marian Anderson
1897-1993
African-American Classical, Opera, and Spiritual Singer
First African-American to Perform with the Metropolitan Opera

MARIAN ANDERSON WAS BORN on February 17, 1897, in Philadelphia, Pennsylvania. Her parents were John and Anna Anderson. John sold ice and coal. Anna was a teacher before she had children. Marian was the oldest of three girls. Her two younger sisters were named Alyce and Ethel.

MARIAN ANDERSON GREW UP in a loving, nurturing home. She grew up loving music, and started to sing at three. She remembered "beating out some sort of rhythm with my hands and feet and la-la-la-ing a vocal accompaniment. Some people might say that these were the first signs of music in me. I would only say that I felt cozy and happy."

Marian's family attended the Union Baptist Church in Philadelphia. She began to sing in the church choir at age six. When she was eight, she earned her first fee. She was paid 50 cents to sing at church. Flyers circulated in the neighborhood, saying: "Come and hear the baby contralto."

"Contralto" refers to a particular range in the signing voice. There are four parts in traditional vocal music. They are soprano, alto, tenor, and bass. In her career, Marian sang as a contralto, which is between alto and tenor.

Yet, even as a child, Anderson could sing higher and lower than the traditional contralto range. She could sing an incredible three full octaves. That's 24 notes in sequence, from lowest to highest pitch. By the time she was 13, she was singing in the adult choir. If any of the soloists in any voice part couldn't perform, Marian would sing the part.

She played instruments, too. She studied piano, and, after scrubbing steps for five cents per job, she saved enough to buy a violin for $3.98. She played it until it fell apart.

A FAMILY TRAGEDY: When Marian was just 12 years old, her beloved father died of a brain tumor. The family had to move in with her father's parents. It was a difficult time. Anderson recalled feeling that "tragedy had moved into our house." Her grandmother was strong-willed and domineering. She was "used to being the boss of her own house and the people in it," Anderson wrote later.

Her mother went to work as a domestic laborer, and also took in laundry. Marian and her sisters helped out any way they could. Anderson was devoted to her mother. She credited her mother with giving her the strength to face all the challenges in life.

MARIAN ANDERSON WENT TO SCHOOL at the local public schools in Philadelphia. She did well in school, and remembered liking spelling bees and speech classes. She started high school at William Penn High, a commercial high school. She took typing and shorthand, courses designed to help her find an office job.

But the focus of her schooling soon changed. An important community member heard Marian sing a solo at a school concert. He thought a young woman of her talent should be taking college preparatory courses. He also thought she should be studying music. Anderson transferred to South Philadelphia High School. There, she began taking more challenging courses and studying music.

FACING RACISM: When she was 15, Anderson first faced the racist attitudes that frequently threatened her career. She tried to apply to a music school, but was rejected. "We don't take colored," the school clerk told her.

The words stung. "It was my first contact with the blunt, brutal words. This school of music was the last place I expected to hear them. True enough, my skin was different, but not my feelings." As she would do throughout her career, Anderson refused to let the bigoted views of others define her.

SERIOUS TRAINING: Anderson first began to study music seriously at 15. A well-known singer and teacher named Mary Patterson accepted her as a student, and her vocal training began in earnest.

Serious vocal training begins with developing technique. Anderson learned how to breathe properly. She did scale studies and other exercises to develop the strength and flexibility of her voice. She studied the correct pronunciations of words from several languages—English, German, French, and Latin.

Anderson loved the training, and worked hard. She knew she needed the foundation of solid technique.

*Anderson performing on the steps of the
Lincoln Memorial, April 9, 1939.*

"The purpose of all the exercises and labors was to give
you a thoroughly reliable foundation and to make sure
you could do your job under any circumstances. There
is no shortcut," she said.

STARTING A CAREER IN MUSIC: Anderson began performing in the Philadelphia area while she was still in
high school. When she'd get paid, she'd give most of the
money to her mother. She also began to study with a
well-known teacher named Giuseppe Boghetti. He
helped her develop the songs and sound that made her
an international star.

Anderson began to study the *lieder* (LEE-der), or songs, of great composers like Franz Schubert and Johannes Brahms. They require outstanding technique, but also emotional power. They often tell a story, and are set to folktales or poems. Anderson brought out the sensitivity and beauty at the heart of these great songs. She also performed famous arias from operas by composers like Mozart and Verdi.

She was also known for her beautiful performances of spirituals. In songs like "My Lord, What a Morning" she brought to life, and celebrated, an African-American art form.

Anderson began to tour the country. She earned enough to buy a house for her mother and sisters. In 1923, she won a vocal competition in Philadelphia. She was the first African-American ever to win the contest. In 1925, she won a national competition. Her prize was the chance to perform with the great New York Philharmonic Orchestra. Her concert was a tremendous hit.

SINGING IN EUROPE: Anderson decided to travel to Europe to study and perform. She was a sensation. While touring Finland, she met the famous classical composer Sibelius. She visited him at his home, where she sang one of his pieces. "My roof is too low for you," he exclaimed.

In Austria, the great conductor Arturo Toscanini heard her sing. "Yours is a voice such as one hears once in a hundred years!" he told her.

Anderson performs at the January 1943 dedication of the mural depicting her 1939 concert.

Anderson returned to the U.S. in triumph. She began a national tour in New York City. Her schedule was hectic: she gave up to 100 concerts each year. She became a true national treasure. She was adored for her beautiful voice and artistry, and her humble, dignified manner.

SINGING AT THE WHITE HOUSE: In 1936, First Lady Eleanor Roosevelt invited Anderson to sing at the White House. She was the first African-American to sing at the President's home.

CONSTITUTION HALL AND THE D.A.R.: In 1939, Anderson became the unlikely center of a controversy. Her manager wanted to book her at Washington D.C.'s Constitution Hall. The Hall is run by the D.A.R. (Daughters of the American Revolution). It is a conservative women's

Anderson at her Metropolitan Opera debut, Jan. 7, 1955.

group that, in 1939, would not allow African-Americans to perform.

First Lady Eleanor Roosevelt, a member of the D.A.R. was outraged. She quit the organization. Harold Ickes, then Interior Secretary, arranged to have Anderson perform at the Lincoln Memorial. It was one of the most memorable concerts ever heard in the nation's capitol.

THE LINCOLN MEMORIAL CONCERT: On Easter Sunday, April 9, 1939, Anderson stood on the steps of the Lincoln Memorial and sang to a crowd of 75,000. Among them were Supreme Court justices, members of Congress, and Civil Rights and religious leaders.

Anderson walked to the platform, closed her eyes, and began to sing "America." She sang Schubert lieder, opera arias, and closed with spirituals. A hush fell over the audience. It was, in the words of one spectator, "a silence instinctive, natural, and intense, so that you were afraid to breathe."

"What were my own feelings?" Anderson wrote later about the controversy. "I was saddened and ashamed. I was sorry for the people who had precipitated the affair. I felt that their behavior stemmed from a lack of understanding. They were not persecuting me personally or as a representative of my people so much as they were doing something that was neither sensible nor good."

FIGHTING PREJUDICE IN THE CONCERT HALL: Anderson was a private woman. "I was not designed for hand-to-hand combat," she said. But she continued to confront and overcome prejudice wherever she could. While touring the South, she came face to face with the racism that limited the lives of African-Americans. It was the time of Jim Crow laws. Businesses—hotels, restaurants, concert halls— could legally discriminate against black people.

But when Anderson performed in the South, she refused to allow the segregated seating that was legal under Jim Crow. At that time, African-Americans could be forced to sit in segregated, inferior areas. She insisted instead that African-Americans be able to sit in every section of a performance hall.

SINGING AT THE METROPOLITAN OPERA: Anderson broke another racial barrier in the 1950s. On January 7, 1955, she became the first African-American to perform with the Metropolitan Opera, one of the most important opera companies in the world. When she appeared on stage, the audience gave her a standing ovation, before she sang a single note.

Anderson sang at the inauguration of President Dwight D. Eisenhower in 1957. President Eisenhower asked her to become a musical ambassador for the U.S.

Anderson traveled the world, singing and bringing the beauty and dignity of her music to thousands. Eisenhower also named her to the United Nations Human Rights Committee.

In 1961, Anderson sang at another presidential inauguration, this time for John F. Kennedy. In 1964, she began her farewell tour. She started at Constitution Hall, and finished in New York's Carnegie Hall. After she retired, she frequently appeared at charity fund raisers for organizations like the NAACP.

Anderson also founded a scholarship given each year to a young singer. It has helped launch the careers of such great African-American singers as Grace Bumbry.

MARIAN ANDERSON'S HOME AND FAMILY: Anderson married Orpheus Fisher in 1943. They had no children. They lived on a 100-acre farm in rural Connecticut. Fisher died in 1986. Anderson developed heart disease and moved to Portland, Oregon, to live with her nephew. She died in Portland on April 8, 1993.

Marian Anderson was one of the greatest musical artists of the 20th century. She was also a courageous figure in the struggle for equal opportunity for African-Americans. At the time of her death, the opera star Jess-eye Norman paid tribute to her. "Marian Anderson was the personification of all that is wonderful, simple, pure, and majestic in the human spirit. She wore the glorious crown of her voice with the grace of an empress."

WORLD WIDE WEB SITES:

http://www.library.upenn.edu/exhibits/rbm/anderson/index.html

http://www.lkwdpl.org/wihohio/ande-mar.htm

http://www.mariananderson.org/legacy/

Romare Bearden
1911 - 1988
African-American Artist

ROMARE BEARDEN WAS BORN on September 2, 1911, in Charlotte, North Carolina. His parents were Richard Howard and Bessye Bearden. His father was a pianist who worked in the Department of Health in New York City. His mother was a journalist and also founded the Negro Women's Democratic Association. Romare was an only child.

ROMARE BEARDEN GREW UP first in the rural South. He remembered the field hands working in the fields, the women cooking, the trains going by. Even after the family moved North, Romare spent summers in the South with his grandparents.

Romare's parents were both college educated and middle class. They knew that opportunities for African-Americans were limited in the South. It was the time of Jim Crow. Legalized segregation limited opportunities for African-Americans, in everything from education to jobs. So they decided to move North.

When Romare was three, the family moved to Harlem, in New York City. It would become an important influence on his life and work. Harlem was the center of African-American art, music, and literature. It was the time of the Harlem Renaissance. His parents knew some of the greatest musicians of the time. Bearden remembered Duke Ellington playing piano duets with his dad.

When he was 13, Romare was sent to live with his grandmother in Pittsburgh, Pennsylvania. She ran a boarding house, and Romare enjoyed getting to know the boarders. He also made a new friend, Eugene, who encouraged him to draw. He especially loved to draw cartoons.

ROMARE BEARDEN WENT TO SCHOOL first in New York, then in Pittsburgh. He attended P.S. 139 in Harlem. In Pittsburgh, he attended Peabody High School. He was a good student, and an athlete, too. He played baseball so well that he played pro ball as an adult.

After graduating from high school, Bearden went on to college at Lincoln University. He transferred to Boston University, where he was art director of the student magazine, *Beanpot*. Bearden transferred again, to New York University, where he worked as a cartoonist and art editor for a college magazine. While still in college, he began to draw magazine covers. He graduated with a degree in education.

Bearden continued to study art after college. He attended the Art Students League in New York, and also the Sorbonne, a famous university in France. He kept his hand in cartooning, too. For several years he was the editorial cartoonist for a black newspaper, the *Baltimore Afro-American*.

INFLUENCES: In the 1930s, Bearden met other African-American artists, including Jacob Lawrence. He met famous writers like Langston Hughes and Ralph Ellison. He learned much from them, and shared their devotion to creating a uniquely African-American art.

Bearden joined the Harlem Artists Guild. He studied early European artists, like Giotto, and 20th century masters like Picasso. He learned all he could about the art of all cultures, including African art.

FIRST JOBS: After college, Bearden worked as a social worker with New York City. He worked in that job for 30 years, painting at night. By 1940, he was ready to exhibit his work.

STARTING TO SHOW HIS PAINTINGS: In 1940, Bearden held his first art show in Harlem. When the U.S. entered World War II in 1941, Bearden served his country and put his art career on hold.

During World War II, Bearden served in the Army. He was part of an all-black brigade. After the war, Bearden toured Europe. He studied literature and philosophy, and visited museums, absorbing all he could about art.

Bearden returned to the U.S. In 1944, he had his first national show, in Washington D.C. He was beginning to gain a reputation for his work.

CELEBRATING THE AFRICAN-AMERICAN EXPERIENCE IN ART: From his earliest work, Bearden wanted to celebrate the life of black Americans. He became known for his collage technique.

In works like *The Block,* Bearden used fabric, painting, ink, and photographs to show his vision of street life in Harlem. *The Block* features a series of row houses. Each of the six panels in the work shows a different group of people. There are family scenes and religious scenes. There is joy and sorrow. There are homeless people and people with happy homes. Bearden shows all walks of life, celebrating and sharing in those lives.

The Block; *Art © Romare Bearden/Licensed by VAGA, New York, NY.*

Bearden was involved in the Civil Rights Movement, too. Along with other artists, he founded a group called Spiral, an organization of African-American artists who worked for equal rights. In 1984, on the 30th anniversary of Brown v. the Board of Education, Bearden created a lithograph, *The Lamp*, to commemorate the end of segregation in the schools. (Brown v. the Board of Education was a Supreme Court case. It ended legal segregation in the schools and other public facilities.)

Sometimes Bearden remembered the South of his youth in his art. In works like *Tomorrow I'll be Far Away* he shows a figure full of love for home, but yearning for more. This work is also a collage. Bearden used magazine clippings, wallpaper, spray paint, and charcoal to achieve his vision.

The Block; *Art © Romare Bearden/Licensed by VAGA, New York, NY.*

Bearden worked in many different art mediums and styles. He did collage, watercolor, and oil painting. He also created photo montages and prints. Bearden explored other art forms, too. He created costumes and sets for the ballets of Alvin Ailey. His wife, Nanette Rohan, was a dancer and choreographer. He created designs for her company, too.

Bearden also did book illustrations, magazine covers, album covers, and sculpture. He even wrote music. One of his songs, "Sea Breeze," became a hit recording for jazz greats Billy Eckstine, Oscar Pettiford, and Dizzy Gillespie. Bearden was an artist of great gifts, which he shared in many different art forms.

Bearden was also devoted to helping young African-American artists. He directed the Harlem Cultural

The Lamp; *Art © Romare Bearden/Licensed by VAGA, New York, NY.*

Council. He also helped found The Studio Museum and the Cinque Gallery. Those were places where young artists could show their work and get recognized.

ROMARE BEARDEN'S HOME AND FAMILY: Bearden married Nanette Rohan in 1954. In addition to their home in New York, they had a house on the Caribbean island of St. Martin, where Nanette's parents had been born. Romare Bearden died on March 12, 1988, in New York City. He was 76 years old.

Bearden is considered one of the most important artists of the 20th century. He reflected his love for African-American life in his art. He told the story of every-day life of black Americans in his art, to the rhythms and spirit of jazz music. He was also devoted to helping young artists develop their talents. Today, his works are displayed in some of the country's most important museums.

FOR MORE INFORMATION:

Write: Romare Bearden Foundation
　　　 305 Seventh Avenue
　　　 New York, NY 10001

WORLD WIDE WEB SITES:
http://www.beardenfoundation.org
http://www.metmuseum.org/
http://www.nga.gov/cgi-bin/pbio?246170

C. S. Lewis
1898-1963
British Essayist, Novelist, and Scholar
Creator of *The Chronicles of Narnia*

C. S. LEWIS WAS BORN on November 29, 1898, in Belfast, Northern Ireland. His full name was Clive Staples Lewis, and he was always known as Jack. His parents were Albert and Flora Lewis. Albert was a lawyer and Flora was a homemaker. Jack had one brother, Warren, called Warnie.

C. S. LEWIS GREW UP in the Belfast area. He wrote of his childhood: "I am the product of long corridors, empty

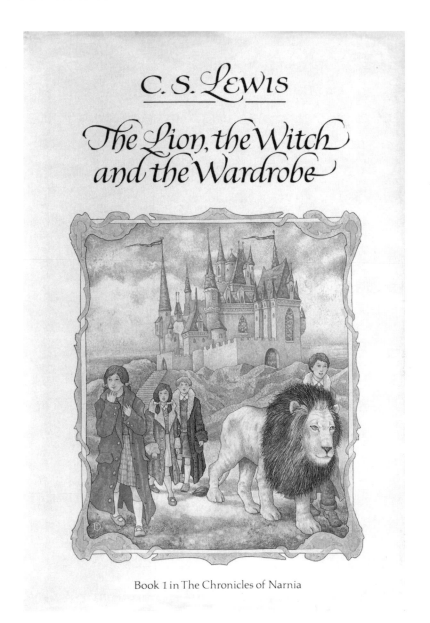

Book 1 in The Chronicles of Narnia

sunlit rooms, upstairs indoor silences, attics explored in solitude, and the noise of wind under the tiles."

His parents were book lovers, and he remembers a house full of them. "There were books in the study, books in the drawing-room, books in the cloakroom, books (two deep) in the great bookcase on the landing, books in the bedroom, books of all kinds, books readable and unreadable, books suitable for a child and books most emphatically not. Nothing was forbidden me. In the seemingly endless rainy afternoons, I took volume after volume from the shelves." He especially loved fairy tales, myths, and Norse sagas.

But his life changed suddenly when he was nine. His beloved mother died, and he and his brother were sent to school in England.

C. S. LEWIS WENT TO SCHOOL first in England, where he attended Wynyard School. Two years later, he became ill and went home to Belfast to get better. There, he attended Campbell College. After he recovered, he went back to England and attended Cherbourg School in Malvern.

Lewis was a brilliant student in nearly all subjects except math. He was especially good at languages, and studied Latin, Greek, French, German, and Italian.

OXFORD AND WAR: Lewis went to Oxford University for college in 1917. He spent only a few months there. World War I had broken out in 1914. That conflict pitted England and France against Germany. By 1917, millions of people had died in the war.

Lewis enlisted in the army and was sent to France in November 1917. He was wounded in April 1918 and sent

back to England. Like many people of his generation, Lewis lost friends in the war. One of his closest friends, Paddy Moore, was killed in 1918.

Lewis returned to Oxford and completed his degree. He was an outstanding student, and received honors at his graduation. In 1925, he began teaching at Magdalen College in Oxford. It was the beginning of an outstanding career as a scholar and writer that lasted nearly 40 years.

A BRILLIANT SCHOLAR: Lewis became known as one of the most gifted scholars of his day. He published books on literary topics, including studies of medieval literature and art. But he was perhaps best known as the most important writer of his time on Christianity.

A RELIGIOUS CONVERSION: When Lewis was 34 years old, he had a profound religious experience. As a young adult, he had rejected his religious upbringing and belief. Then, one day, he felt the presence of God. He described it as "the steady, unrelenting approach of Him whom I so earnestly desired not to meet." Then, he wrote later, "I gave in, and admitted that God was God, and knelt and prayed."

Lewis's conversion changed his life and his work. He began writing on the meaning of Christian faith. He gave speeches, and read his work on the radio, gaining millions of listeners in England. Readers throughout the world read his essays on belief. Even though he was an academic man, Lewis's writings on faith were simple, direct, and profound. He touched the hearts and minds of many people.

THE INKLINGS: Lewis was good friends with a group of other Oxford professors, including J. R. R. Tolkien, the

author of *The Lord of the Rings.* Lewis, Tolkien, Owen Barfield, his brother Warnie, and others used to meet regularly to discuss their current work. They called themselves "the Inklings." It was among these friends that Lewis discussed the work for which he is best known to young readers, *The Chronicles of Narnia.*

THE CHRONICLES OF NARNIA: Lewis published his *Narnia* series in seven volumes, from 1950 to 1956. Since then, they have become some of the most beloved children's books ever written.

The Lion, the Witch, and the Wardrobe: The first book in the series is *The Lion, the Witch, and the Wardrobe*. It features the adventures of four children who are sent to live in the country during the war. The four children—Peter, Susan, Edmund, and Lucy—are playing one day when Lucy makes an amazing discovery. Through the back of the wardrobe, she leaves the everyday world and enters the land of Narnia. It is one of the most amazing fantasy worlds in all literature.

In Narnia, the children find talking animals and other incredible creatures. They encounter the White Witch, a figure of brutal cruelty, who holds Narnia captive in an endless winter. And they meet the miraculous Aslan, King of the Beasts. In the course of their adventures, they learn the true meaning of loyalty, friendship, and sacrifice, embodied in the mighty Aslan.

Prince Caspian: In the second Narnia book, the children are called upon again. They return to Narnia to help Prince Caspian, whose uncle, the evil Miraz, has taken his throne. They must gather troops again, this time to defeat Miraz and restore Prince Caspian to his rightful position.

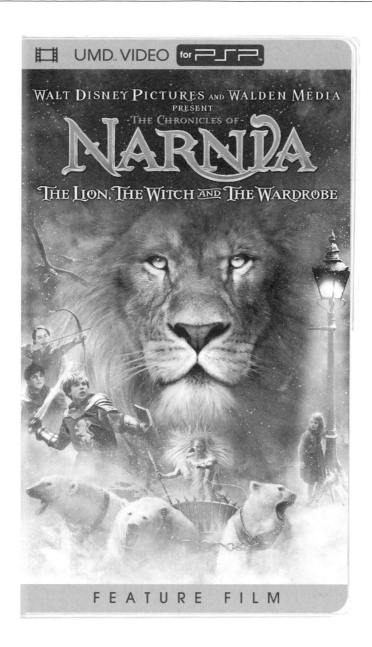

The Voyage of the Dawn Treader: The third book in the series features Lucy and Edmund entering Narnia through a picture, along with their cousin Eustace Scrubb. They join Caspian, now king, in his quest to find his loyal subjects who had been banished by Miraz.

The Silver Chair: In the fourth book, Eustace and his friend Jill Pole escape from school bullies and enter Narnia, through a strange door. They must help find Prince Rilian, who is being held by an evil witch and bound to a silver chair. With Aslan's aid, they save the prince, and Narnia, again.

The Horse and His Boy: The fifth Narnia book features Peter as High King, and new characters. One is a boy, Shasta, who runs away from home, seeking his true father. He enters Narnia, and is helped in his quest by Aravis, a girl of bravery and daring.

The Magician's Nephew: *The Magician's Nephew* was the sixth Narnia book to appear. But Lewis wanted readers to read it first, because it tells the story of the creation of Narnia. The two main characters are Digory and Polly. They enter the world that will become Narnia, and battle a witch.

The Last Battle: The final book in the series is *The Last Battle*. It is about the final conflict between good and evil, and the end of Narnia. Aslan's last words are: "The dream is ended: this is the morning."

The Chronicles of Narnia have delighted readers for more than 50 years. Young readers thrill to the adventures they find in the books. Older readers love the story, as well as the novels' deep moral and philosophical richness. The Narnia books are some of the most popular and widely-read books of all time. And in 2005, they came alive on the screen.

THE MOVIE VERSION: In 2005, *The Lion, the Witch,* and the *Wardrobe* was made into a movie. It was very successful, and drew many new readers to Lewis's classic children's series. The next film in the series, *Prince Caspian*, appears in 2008. The films' success reflect the timelessness of Lewis's fables of faith, wonder, and fantasy.

C. S. LEWIS'S HOME AND FAMILY: In the 1950s, Lewis met Joy Davidman Gresham. She was an American scholar. They married in 1956. Tragically, Joy died of cancer in 1960. Lewis was the stepfather of her son, Douglas Gresham. C. S. Lewis died on November 22, 1963.

THE CHRONICLES OF NARNIA:

The Magician's Nephew
The Lion, the Witch, and the Wardrobe
The Horse and His Boy
Prince Caspian
The Voyage of the Dawn Treader
The Silver Chair
The Last Battle

*Note: Although this is not the order in which Lewis wrote the books, it is the order in which he wanted them to be read.

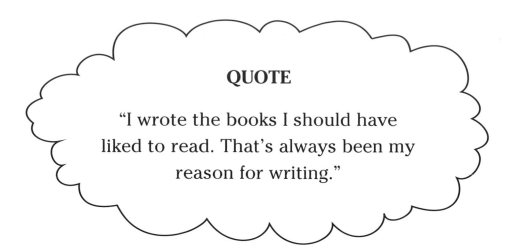

QUOTE

"I wrote the books I should have liked to read. That's always been my reason for writing."

FOR MORE INFORMATION:

Write: HarperCollins Children's Books
1350 Avenue of the Americas
New York, NY 10019

WORLD WIDE WEB SITES:

http://cslewis.drzeus.net/
http://www.cslewis.org
http://www.harpercollinschildrens.com/
http://www.narnia.com

Anita Lobel
1934-
Polish-Born American Author and Illustrator
of Books for Children

ANITA LOBEL WAS BORN on June 2, 1934, in Cracow, Poland. Her last name became Lobel when she married. Her name when she was born was Anita Kempler. Her parents were Leon and Sofia Kempler. She had one brother.

ANITA LOBEL GREW UP in Poland under the specter of war. Her family was Jewish. Anita's parents watched in horror as the Nazi party, under Adolf Hitler, rose to power in neighboring Germany. Hitler and the Nazis believed that all Jews were inferior.

As the threat of war grew, Anita's parents separated and fled Poland. They left their children in the care of their nanny. She was Catholic, and was able to pass the children off as her own, for a while.

WORLD WAR II AND LIFE IN A CONCENTRATION CAMP: World War II took place between 1939 and 1945 in Europe, Africa, and the Far East. In the war, Germany, Italy, and Japan made up the "Axis" powers. They fought against the "Allies"—England, France, and the Soviet Union. The U.S. joined in the war in 1941, after Japan attacked Pearl Harbor.

In 1939, Germany declared war on Poland and invaded. Anita, her brother, and their nanny fled Cracow. For five years, they escaped capture by the Nazis. On Christmas Day in 1944, the Nazis found them, hiding in a convent. Anita and her brother were sent to prison, then to a concentration camp.

The reality of the Nazi regime is horrifying. They killed millions of people during World War II, including more than six million Jews. Somehow, Anita and her brother survived the concentration camps.

Lobel credits her beloved nanny with giving her the strength and love to go on. "Aside from the fact that there was an outside force that hated us and chased us,

I always felt my brother and I were protected by this person. I really feel Nanny's affection colors my work, because I don't feel I have to portray the awful bleakness of the time." In fact, it wasn't until 1998 that she told the story of her early life, in a book titled *No Pretty Pictures: A Child of War.*

In 1945, the Swedish Red Cross rescued the children. They were taken to Sweden and reunited with their parents. Finally, Anita and her family could live a normal life.

LIFE IN SWEDEN: In Sweden, Anita discovered books and the theater. She went to high school and began to draw.

MOVING TO THE UNITED STATES: In 1952, the Kempler family moved to the U.S. They settled in New York City. Anita decided to follow her passion for art.

ART SCHOOL: In New York, Anita attended Pratt Institute. That is one of the finest art schools in the country. She always had a love of theater, and one day, she landed a role in a play directed by a student named Arnold Lobel. They fell in love and married in 1955.

FIRST JOBS: After graduating from Pratt, Lobel started to work in fabric design. Her husband, Arnold, began to write and illustrate books for children, including the beloved *Frog and Toad* series. Anita, too, tried her hand at creating children's books. She discovered she loved it.

SVEN'S BRIDGE: Lobel's first book was *Sven's Bridge*. She created the art work first, basing it on folk designs from Sweden. Then, after the pictures were complete, she recalls, "the words followed."

WORKING WITH ARNOLD LOBEL: Anita and Arnold Lobel created several award-winning books together. In 1977, they collaborated on their first book, *How the Rooster Saved the Day.*

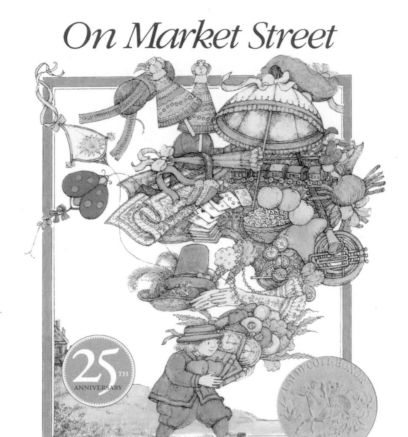

On Market Street

Pictures by Anita Lobel
Words by Arnold Lobel

ON MARKET STREET: One of the Lobels' most successful co-creations was *On Market Street*. It is an ABC book, and follows a child visiting all the stores on Market Street. Anita Lobel's lively illustrations feature people made of books, doughnuts, gloves, noodles, even zippers. The Lobels won a Caldecott Honor for the work. That's one of the most prized honors in children's literature.

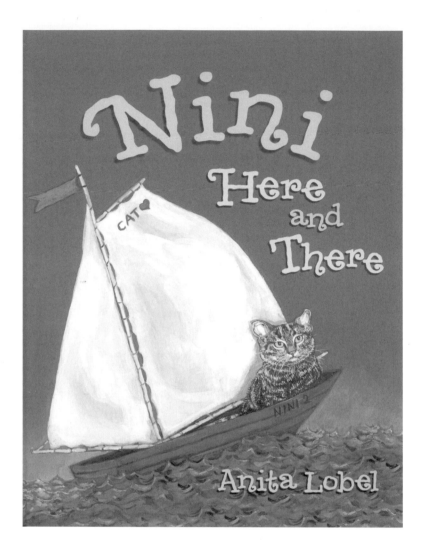

THE ROSE IN MY GARDEN: The Lobels final work together was *The Rose in My Garden*. The words and the brilliantly colored pictures tell the story of all the plants and creatures in a garden. All seems calm and happy until a cat intrudes. But all ends well, and order is restored, even if the cat has to deal with a bee sting.

Since Arnold Lobel's death in 1987, Anita Lobel has continued to write and illustrate her own books, and to illustrate books for other authors. "My own texts usually grow out of pictures that I want to paint," she says.

Lobel recently illustrated Kevin Henkes's *So Happy!* The two authors enjoyed working together. Lobel said this about illustrating another author's work: "I find great pleasure in making visible the unexpected layer of content in a story. I want to get it right, and I hope I have fun surprising the author as well."

NINI HERE AND THERE: One of Lobel's most recent books is *Nini Here and There*. It features her cat, Nini, traveling, dreaming, and, at last, enjoying her summer vacation with her family.

ANITA LOBEL'S HOME AND FAMILY: Anita and Arnold Lobel married in 1955. They had two children, Adrienne and Adam. Arnold Lobel died in 1987, at the age of 53.

Anita Lobel continues to live and work in New York and at her summer home in Vermont. She also exhibits her art in galleries and museums around the U.S.

SOME OF ANITA LOBEL'S BOOKS:

As Author and Illustrator
Sven's Bridge
Potatoes, Potatoes
Alison's Zinnia
Animal Antics: A to Z
Nini Here and There

> **QUOTE**
>
> "It is the 'drama' in a picture book that interests me most. I stage the story the way a director might work on a theater piece."

As Illustrator

How the Rooster Saved the Day
A Treeful of Pigs
On Market Street
A Rose in My Garden
The Night before Christmas
This Quiet Lady
All the World's a Stage
So Happy!

FOR MORE INFORMATION ABOUT ANITA LOBEL:

Write: Greenwillow Books
1350 Avenue of the Americas
New York, NY 10010

WORLD WIDE WEB SITES:

http://www.anitalobel.com

http://www.harpercollins.com/authors/17469/Anita_Lobel/index.htm

http://www.teachingk-8.com/archives/author_interview/anita_lobel

Eli Manning
1981-
American Professional Football Player
with the New York Giants
Most Valuable Player of the 2008 Super Bowl

ELI MANNING WAS BORN on January 3, 1981, in New
Orleans, Louisiana. His full name is Elisha Nelson Manning.
His father, Archie Manning, was a football star. He played
14 seasons in the National Football League (NFL). For most
of his professional career, Archie was the quarterback of
the New Orleans Saints. Eli's mother, Olivia Manning, was a

homemaker. He has two older brothers, Cooper and Peyton, who were both talented football players.

ELI MANNING GREW UP in an active, athletic family. He was quiet and shy as a boy. He sometimes found it hard to compete with his big brothers. "I got pounded on a little bit," he admitted. "At the time I didn't really enjoy it, but it made me tough."

ELI MANNING WENT TO SCHOOL in New Orleans at Isidore Newman High School. He was a star quarterback on the school's football team. Many college teams recruited him. Eli decided to attend the University of Mississippi (known as Ole Miss). Both his father and his brother Cooper had played college football there.

Eli attended Ole Miss from 1999 to 2004. Like his father, he played quarterback for the school's football team. Eli passed for more than 10,000 yards during his college career. He also accounted for 86 career touchdowns. This total broke the school record of 56 that had been set by his father. All together, Eli set 47 game, season, and career records at Ole Miss. He won the Maxwell Award and the Johnny Unitas Golden Arm Award during his senior season.

DRAFTED INTO THE NFL: The San Diego Chargers selected Manning first overall in the 2004 NFL draft. But Manning refused to play for the Chargers. The team had not performed well for a few seasons. Still, Manning's decision upset many people. They felt that it was selfish and unfair. "I didn't think San Diego was the place for me to go," he explained. "It was my decision, and I felt strongly about it. I knew I was going to get criticized and harassed about it, and I was willing to go through that."

A few days after the draft, the Chargers traded Manning to the New York Giants. The Giants gave up a lot to get Manning. They sent quarterback Philip Rivers, who had been selected fourth overall in the draft, and three other high draft picks to the Chargers. Since the Giants paid such a high price for Manning, New York fans wanted the rookie quarterback to play well right away. In fact, they expected Eli to be as good as his brother Peyton.

Peyton Manning had been drafted first overall in 1998 by the Indianapolis Colts. By the time Eli entered the NFL, Peyton was one of the best quarterbacks in the league. He eventually earned two NFL Most Valuable Player awards and led the Colts to victory in the 2007 Super Bowl. But Eli did not mind being compared with his older brother. "I consider it a compliment," he said. "If I'm getting compared to one of the best quarterbacks in the league, that's a good position to be in. I'm trying to reach his level of play, get to that position."

ROOKIE SEASON: Eli Manning struggled during his first year with the Giants. He became the team's starting quarterback in November 2004. But New York lost the first six games he started. Manning did not earn his first NFL victory until the last game of the season.

Many Giants fans were upset when the team ended the 2004 season with a 6-10 record. Manning knew he had not lived up to expectations. He turned to Peyton for advice and support. "It's rare to have a best friend who is also your brother and also an NFL football player," Eli explained, "and he knows exactly what I'm talking about."

HELPING OUT AFTER HURRICANE KATRINA: As the 2005 NFL season got underway, a natural disaster struck Manning's hometown. Hurricane Katrina destroyed much of New Orleans and forced many residents to leave the city. The Manning family had to move to Mississippi.

Eli and Peyton wanted to do something to help people who lost their homes. They sent an airplane full of food, clothing, and other supplies to New Orleans. "It's hard to watch what's happened to the city, people with no place to go, up to their waists in water," Eli recalled. "We just wanted to do something extra, so we set up this plan to help some of these people."

THE 2005 SEASON: The Giants had a good season in 2005. They won the NFL East Division title with an 11-5 record. Manning passed for 3,762 yards and 24 touchdowns. But the young quarterback also made lots of

Manning throws a pass during a playoff game against Tampa Bay, Jan. 6, 2008.

mistakes. He threw 20 interceptions during the regular season. Manning's worst game came in the first round of the playoffs. He threw 3 interceptions, took 4 sacks, and lost a fumble against the Carolina Panthers. The Giants lost the game 23-0.

THE 2006 SEASON: At the start of the 2006 season, the Manning family made history. The Giants played the Colts in the first game of the year. Eli and Peyton became the first brothers ever to start at quarterback for opposing teams in an NFL game. The Giants lost the game and ended up with a disappointing 8-8 record. Manning played well at times, but the young quarterback struggled in other games. Many New York fans blamed him for the team's failure to make the playoffs.

THE 2007 SEASON: By the start of the 2007 season, some people wondered whether Manning would ever develop into a top NFL quarterback. He even faced criticism from fellow players, like former Giants running back Tiki Barber. Barber told reporters that Manning was too quiet and low-key to inspire his teammates. He questioned Manning's ability to lead the Giants.

Manning tried not to let such comments bother him. He kept working hard to prove the critics wrong. "You just have to learn to accept it," he stated. "You can't let it affect your personality or the way you are in the locker room or your approach. You have to stay the same and have a good attitude about everything and show everybody that it doesn't bother you and doesn't affect you and you are going to go out there and still practice hard and perform hard."

Manning continued to struggle during the regular season. He tied for worst in the league with 20 interceptions. But the young quarterback also showed flashes of greatness. He led the Giants to a 10-6 record and a wild card spot in the 2007 NFL playoffs.

THE 2007 PLAYOFFS: As a wild card team, the Giants had to win three tough playoff games on the road to reach the Super Bowl. These were some of the best games of Manning's career. He showed great patience and confidence, and he made very few mistakes. Manning's outstanding play helped his team make an amazing playoff run.

First, the Giants faced the Tampa Bay Buccaneers in the wild card game. Manning completed 20 of 27 passes for 185 yards, 2 touchdowns, and no interceptions. His strong performance led New York to a 24-14 victory. The next week the Giants played the Dallas Cowboys for the division title. The Cowboys felt confident because they had beaten New York twice during the regular season. But Manning took control of the Giants' offense and led his team to a 21-17 victory.

The National Football Conference (NFC) Championship game took place in Green Bay, Wisconsin. The Giants and the Packers played in terrible January weather. The players endured heavy snow, extreme cold, and high winds during the game. But Manning did not let the conditions bother him. The young quarterback rallied his team to an exciting 23-20 overtime win.

Manning scrambles to set up the winning play of the Super Bowl, Feb. 3, 2008.

THE SUPER BOWL: Manning and his teammates were thrilled to reach the Super Bowl. But they knew that no one expected them to win. Their opponents were the New England Patriots. Led by superstar quarterback Tom Brady, the Patriots had gone undefeated in the 2007 season. Many people considered them to be one of the best teams in NFL history.

The Giants played tough during the Super Bowl. They held the powerful Patriots offense to 14 points. Still, New York trailed 14-10 with just over a minute left in the game. Manning stayed calm and moved his team down the field. The key play of the final drive came on third down at the Giants' 44 yard line. Manning dropped back to pass and found himself surrounded by New England defenders. It looked like he would be tackled for a sack.

Manning celebrates the Giants' victory in the Super Bowl, with TV commentator Terry Bradshaw and coach Tom Coughlin.

To the shock of football fans everywhere, Manning somehow got away. Then he launched a 32-yard pass to receiver David Tyree. Tyree jumped higher than a defender, grabbed the ball with one hand, and trapped it against his helmet for an amazing catch. "I knew people were grabbing me, but I knew I wasn't getting pulled down," Manning recalled. "I was trying to make a play, trying to avoid the sack. I saw [Tyree] in the middle, and the ball just hung up there forever. It was an unbelievable catch."

Manning with his father, Archie, and brother Peyton.

A few plays later, Manning finished the drive with a touchdown pass. The Giants beat the Patriots by a score of 17-14. Stunned reporters called it one of the biggest upsets in NFL history. During the game, Manning completed 19 of 34 passes for 255 yards and 2 touchdowns. His performance earned him the Super Bowl Most Valuable Player Award. It also helped him overcome fans' doubts about his skills and leadership. But Manning insisted that the victory belonged to all the Giants. "This is about this team, about the players, the coaches, everybody who has believed in us," he declared. "It's not about proving anything to anybody. It is just about doing it for yourself, doing it for your teammates."

ELI MANNING'S HOME AND FAMILY: Manning lives in New York. He is engaged to marry his college girlfriend, Abby McGrew, in the spring of 2008. He remains very close to his family, especially his brother Peyton.

QUOTE

"You have to earn respect from your players. You have to figure out what your role is from a leadership standpoint and what you have to do to get your team ready. That just comes from time and proving that you'll make plays, that you can do the right things and put your team in a situation to win."

FOR MORE INFORMATION ABOUT ELI MANNING:

Write: New York Giants
      Attn: Eli Manning
      Giants Stadium
      East Rutherford, NJ 07073

WORLD WIDE WEB SITES:

http://www.giants.com/team/player34.html

http://www.nfl.com/players/elimanning/profile?id=MAN 473170

http://sports.espn.go.com/nfl/players/profile?statsID= 6760

Wilma Rudolph
1940-1994
American Track and Field Athlete
Winner of Three Olympic Gold Medals

WILMA RUDOLPH WAS BORN on June 23, 1940, in St. Bethlehem, Tennessee, about 50 miles from Nashville. Her full name was Wilma Glodean Rudolph. Her parents were Ed and Blanche Rudolph. Blanche worked as a maid. Ed worked as a porter for a railroad company, carrying suitcases for train passengers. He already had 11 children from his first marriage when he met

Blanche. They had nine more children together. Wilma was one of the youngest members of this large family.

Wilma, at right, at age six, with her sister Yvonne.

WILMA RUDOLPH GREW UP in the town of Clarksville, Tennessee. She was often sick as a child. When she was four years old, she caught polio. Polio is a virus that attacks the brain and spinal cord. It causes a high fever and sometimes paralysis (loss of movement). Polio damaged the nerves and muscles in Wilma's left leg. Her doctors worried that she might never be able to walk again.

Wilma wore a heavy metal brace on her leg for many years. Her mother and sisters rubbed her leg every day to make more blood flow to the muscles. One day each week, Wilma and her mother took a bus to Nashville. They went to a city hospital where Wilma learned exercises to strengthen her leg.

GROWING UP IN THE SEGREGATED SOUTH: During these weekly bus trips, Wilma saw the effects of segregation. At this time, segregation laws kept people in the South separated by race. Wilma and other African-Americans were forced to use different waiting areas, bathrooms, and drinking fountains than those used by white people. Black people also had to sit in the back of public buses.

When Wilma was nine years old, she shocked her doctors by walking without her leg brace. She wore special support shoes until she was 11. After that, she was completely healed. "By the time I was 12, I was challenging every boy in our neighborhood at running, jumping, everything," she remembered.

WILMA RUDOLPH WENT TO SCHOOL in Clarksville. Because of her illness, she did not start school until the second grade. She attended two all-black public schools, Cobb Elementary School and Burt High School. As she grew older, Wilma became a star basketball player. She averaged 32 points per game during her sophomore year of high school.

Wilma's speed on the court attracted the attention of Ed Temple. Temple was the women's track coach at Tennessee State University. He told Wilma that she had the talent to be a great runner. He invited her to train with his college team, the Tigerbelles, during the summer. The next year, Wilma joined her high school track team. She never lost a race in two seasons.

RUNNING IN THE 1956 OLYMPICS: Rudolph had never even heard of the Olympics until she met Ed Temple.

Rudolph winning the women's 100-meter dash
at the Rome Olympics, Sept. 2, 1960.

She still managed to qualify for the 1956 Games in Melbourne, Australia. At 16, she was the youngest member of the U.S. team. Rudolph earned a bronze medal by helping the American women finish third in the 400-meter relay race. She knew at that time that she wanted to try for a gold medal in 1960.

In 1958 Rudolph enrolled at Tennessee State. She studied education and joined the Tigerbelles track team. She practiced hard and qualified for three events at the 1960 Olympic Games in Rome, Italy.

1960 OLYMPICS: Rudolph's first event was the 100-meter sprint race. She won the gold medal easily, finishing three meters ahead of her closest competitor. A writer for *Time* magazine said that Rudolph's long, flowing strides "made the rest of the pack seem to be churning on a treadmill." Rudolph earned a second gold medal by winning the 200-meter race.

Then Rudolph joined three of her Tigerbelle teammates—Martha Hudson, Barbara Jones, and Lucinda Williams—in the 400-meter relay race. Each woman ran 100 meters and then passed a baton to the next woman. Rudolph ran the fourth, or anchor, leg of the race. When her turn came, she dropped the baton on the ground. But she picked it up and passed three other runners to claim a third gold medal. Rudolph became the first American woman ever to win three Olympic gold medals in track and field.

BECOMING A STAR: Rudolph's amazing performance at the 1960 Olympics made her a star in Europe and the United States. Many people were touched by the story of how she overcame illness, poverty, and segregation to become the world's fastest woman. Rudolph appeared in parades, gave interviews on television, and even visited President John F. Kennedy at the White House.

When Rudolph returned home to Tennessee, Clarksville officials organized a rally in her honor. But

Rudolph winning the women's 400-meter relay race
at the Rome Olympics, Sept. 8, 1960.

the event they planned was segregated. Rudolph refused to participate if only white people were invited. Town officials were forced to allow black people to attend. The rally attracted 40,000 people. It was the first racially integrated event in the town's history.

Now that she was famous, Rudolph found it hard to go back to her old life. But she could not earn a living as a track star. American companies did not hire black athletes to advertise their products in those days. Rudolph decided that she had to finish her education and get a job. She retired from track in 1963. She earned her college degree and started working as a teacher and coach.

HELPING POOR CHILDREN ENJOY SPORTS: Rudolph learned many important lessons by competing in sports. She wanted to share her experiences with others. She also wanted to help more children from poor families get involved in sports. "My life wasn't like the average person who grew up and decided to enter the world of sports," she explained.

In 1977 Rudolph wrote a book about her life, called *Wilma*. It was turned into a TV movie starring Cicely Tyson and Denzel Washington. Rudolph also gave speeches and helped open sports clinics in cities across the country. In 1981 she started the Wilma Rudolph Foundation to promote amateur sports. Rudolph always taught children the value of working hard to overcome the obstacles in their lives.

WILMA RUDOLPH'S HOME AND FAMILY: Rudolph was married and divorced twice. She had four children: daughters Yolanda and Djuanna, and sons Robert Jr. and Xurry. Rudolph died of a cancerous brain tumor at her home in Brentwood, Tennessee, on November 12, 1994. She was 54 years old.

Rudolph is a symbol of courage and perseverance to generations of athletes, black and white, male and female. She received many awards over the years for her achievements on and off the track. She was a member of the U.S. Olympic Hall of Fame, the National Track and Field Hall of Fame, and the Black Athletes Hall of Fame. Rudolph's image appeared on a U.S. postage stamp, and Tennessee State University named its new track after her. The Women's Sports Foundation created the Wilma Rudolph Courage Award in her honor. It is presented each year to a female athlete who succeeds in the face of challenges.

QUOTE

"The triumph can't be had without the struggle, and I know what struggle is. I have spent a lifetime trying to share what it has meant to be a woman first in the world of sports so that other young women have a chance to reach their dreams."

WORLD WIDE WEB SITES:

http://www.wilmarudolph.net
http://www.lkwdpl.org/wihohio/rudo-wil.htm
http://espn.go.com/sportscentury/features/00016444.html

Schlitz celebrates her Newbery Medal at the Park School,
with a tiara and congratulations from her students.

Laura Amy Schlitz
1955-
American Author, Storyteller, and Librarian
Winner of the Newbery Medal for
Good Masters! Sweet Ladies!

LAURA AMY SCHLITZ WAS BORN in 1955 in Baltimore, Maryland. Her father was a judge's clerk and her mother was a homemaker. She has a brother, Paul.

LAURA AMY SCHLITZ GREW UP in a family that encouraged her love of reading and books. "My parents read to me all through childhood," she recalls. "I can't remember a time when there were no books." She loved fairy tales especially. "I was particularly struck by *Hansel and Gretel* when I was little," she says. "I remember hiding crusts of bread under the dining room table, so that if famine ever struck, I could save the family from starvation."

"I was a lucky child," she says, "because I had a lot of time to play—pretending games, not soccer. I played with dolls and stuffed animals. I was a horse, a panther, a Civil War spy, a witch, a mermaid. I spent a lot of time in the cellar, dressed in mildewy taffeta and old chiffon gowns. I was a happy-go-lucky, curious, vainglorious child." "I haven't changed much," she adds.

LAURA AMY SCHLITZ WENT TO SCHOOL in Baltimore. She has a special memory of learning to read at age six. "I distinctly remember one day reading *Little Bear* to myself and then counting to 100. Then I rocked back and forth in my chair and marveled at my own erudition."

Laura became involved in theater when she was in third grade. She was waiting for her brother to get out of a music lesson when a director saw her. He was struck by her "theatrical" look. She was very small, with long, flowing hair, and seemed wise beyond her years. He cast her in a play. She's performed in plays, and written them, every since.

Schlitz went to Goucher College in Maryland. She studied "aesthetics," a major she created. It included classes in literature, philosophy, and the arts. She recalls her time at Goucher with great affection. "When I remember Goucher, I always have the same picture in my mind. I used to wear long cloaks all winter, and in my memory it's always a windy day. The wind is catching my cloak, and the sky is patched clear blue and cloud-white and the air is full of the sound of crows. I think I picture Goucher this way because I connect those years with a sense of freedom and movement, and of course, with beauty."

FIRST JOBS: After graduating from college, Schlitz got a job at the Enoch Pratt Free Library in Baltimore. She spent eight years there, then left to work full-time for the Baltimore Children's Theater Association.

Schlitz began to write plays for children in the 1980s. They were performed by groups in Maryland and Kentucky.

AUTHOR/LIBRARIAN/STORYTELLER: In 1991, Schlitz took a job at the Park School, a private school in Baltimore. Since then, she's worked as a librarian, storyteller, and writer. Her career as an award-winning author grew out of her work with her students.

One assignment in particular proved to be an inspiration. Schlitz's fifth-graders had an assignment to study life in the Middle Ages. "I wanted them to have something to perform, but no one wanted a small part," she recalls. "So I decided to write monologues instead of

one long play, so that for three minutes at least, every child could be a star."

Those monologues have been performed by Park students since 1997. In 2000, Schlitz sent a manuscript based on the monologues to Candlewick Press. At Candlewick, an editorial assistant found them in the "slush pile." That's where publishers put manuscripts for books that are sent in by unknown authors. She gave Schlitz's manuscript to an editor, Mary Lee Donovan.

Donovan recalls it as "the most exciting submission that I've had in my 23-year career." She loved the book. "My heart definitely beat faster. I was overwhelmed by the clear talent. It was almost a perfect manuscript."

Candlewick accepted the manuscript, as well as three other books by Schlitz. Although the manuscript on the Middle Ages was the first book to be accepted, it was not the first published. That first book was *The Hero Schliemann.* It appeared in 2006.

THE HERO SCHLIEMANN: THE DREAMER WHO DUG UP TROY: *The Hero Schliemann* tells the story of Heinrich Schliemann, a 19th-century German archeologist. Schliemann claimed to have found the original city of Troy, the legendary site of the Trojan War. He is known to some as a hero, and to others as a crook, who exaggerated his accomplishments. In her biography, Schlitz portrays him as flawed but understandable. She says, "Perhaps I'm drawn to slightly nasty people, because I find them easier to understand than the angelic kind."

A DROWNED MAIDEN'S HAIR: Schlitz's second book was *A Drowned Maiden's Hair.* It's the story of an

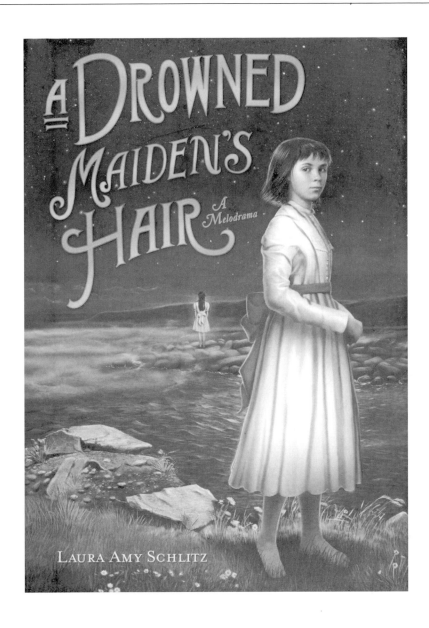

orphan, Maud, who's adopted by the Hawthorne sisters. The sisters pretend to be "mediums," who can contact the dead. Maud is forced to play the ghost of a drowned girl, while the Hawthornes take advantage of grieving people. Schlitz portrays Maud's reaction to the deceit, and the role she's forced to play.

THE BEARSKINNER: A TALE OF THE BROTHERS GRIMM: In her retelling of this Grimms' fairy tale, Schlitz simply and chillingly brings alive the story of a man who bargains with the devil and wins. As the man lives out the terms of his bargain, he gains wisdom and compassion, and the true meaning of loyalty and love. The illustrations, by Max Grafe, add a haunting, timeless feeling to the tale.

GOOD MASTERS! SWEET LADIES! VOICES FROM A MEDIEVAL VILLAGE: The medieval manuscript Schlitz first submitted in 2000 was published in 2007 as *Good Masters! Sweet Ladies! Voices from a Medieval Village*. It quickly became a favorite with readers.

The work is set in England in 1255, and is told in the voices of 22 characters. The speakers are all young people, who come from different levels of medieval society. Whether she's picturing Hugo, the lord's nephew, or Giles, the beggar, Schlitz doesn't spare her readers the reality of the times. The wealthy thrived, the poor starved. They live with death, vermin, and the inequalities of the social system of the time. The monologues are written in different styles, reflecting each individual. Some are in rhyme, some are in simple prose. All are moving and engaging.

Schlitz includes footnotes that explain some of the terms that would be unfamiliar to modern readers. She also has special sections that explain the historical background of the stories, like the farming system, and reli-

gious practices of the times. It is an amazing blend of fiction and nonfiction, created with care and imagination.

WINNING THE NEWBERY MEDAL: In January 2008, Schlitz learned she had won the Newbery Medal for *Good Masters! Sweet Ladies!* That is the most important award in children's literature. When she got to school,

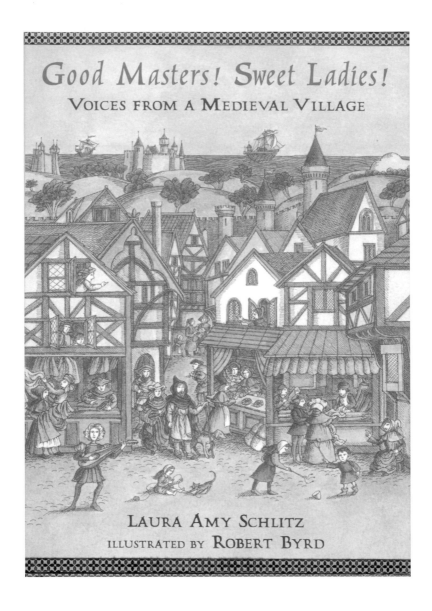

her students and fellow teachers greeted her with a tiara and an assembly in her honor. "I never thought I'd win this award," she told them. "I still can't believe I'd won it. But all the love and loyalty in this room—this is better."

In accepting the award, Schlitz gave special thanks to the Park School. She was able to write the book, in part, because the school gave her a grant that allowed her to research and write. "They have supported my writing in every conceivable way," she says.

FUTURE PLANS: In addition to her work as a librarian and storyteller, Schlitz is working on more books. One, she says, is about a fairy. "My second graders often ask me for 'a book about a fairy', which is quite a different thing from a fairy tale. They want a book in which the fairy is the main character. My fairy-lovers are often quite interesting little girls, and too many fairy books are insipid. So I'm trying to write a 'book about a fairy' that will suit my future wild women of America."

LAURA AMY SCHLITZ'S HOME AND FAMILY: Schlitz, who is single, lives in the Baltimore area.

LAURA AMY SCHLITZ'S BOOKS:
The Hero Schliemann: The Dreamer Who Dug up Troy
A Drowned Maiden's Hair
The Bearskinner: A Tale of the Brothers Grimm
Good Masters! Sweet Ladies! Voices from a Medieval Village

FOR MORE INFORMATION:
Write: Candlewick Press
2067 Massachusetts Ave.
Cambridge, MA 02140

QUOTE

"I'm very lucky to be a school librarian. The children are fantastic. They wake me up and they make me laugh. The knowledge I've gained by telling stories to children is invaluable."

WORLD WIDE WEB SITES:

http://www.baltimoresun.com/news/education/k12/
  bal-te.to.newbery

http://www.candlewick.com

http://www.parkschool.net/

Brian Selznick
1966-
American Children's Author and Illustrator
Winner of the Caldecott Medal for
The Invention of Hugo Cabret

BRIAN SELZNICK WAS BORN in 1966 in New Jersey. He's the oldest of three children and has one sister and one brother.

BRIAN SELZNICK GREW UP loving to draw, and loving movies. He recalls watching monster movies, and trying to create monster costumes. He also loved to draw scenes from films. He still has drawings of Princess Leia and Darth Vader (from *Star Wars*) that he did when he was 10 years old.

BRIAN SELZNICK WENT TO SCHOOL at the local public schools. He always had artistic talent, and his teachers encouraged him. In high school he was encouraged to become a children's book illustrator. But that wasn't in his plans then.

For college, Selznick went to the Rhode Island School of Design, called RISD. That is one of the finest schools of art and design in the country. He thought he wanted to go into theater, so he concentrated on theater and set design. Two of the greatest children's illustrators, Chris Van Allsburg and David Macaulay, teach at RISD. But Brian was devoted to theater, so he didn't take their classes.

After college, Selznick did some traveling. He says he "kept notebooks and drew and wrote stories." When he returned, he got a job that would help launch a brilliant career.

FIRST JOBS: Selznick started to work at Eeyore's Books for Children in New York City. That was one of the best children's book stores in the country. The manager was a man named Steve Geck. Geck introduced Selznick to the wonderful world of children's literature. He sent Brian home with stacks of books every night.

Selznick loved them. He started to work on his own children's book. That first manuscript eventually became *The Houdini Box*. When he was done, he showed it to Geck. Geck showed it to his girlfriend, who was a children's book editor. She wanted to publish it.

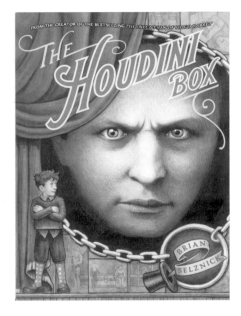

After *The Houdini Box* was published, Selznick stayed on at the bookstore. In addition to selling books, he also gave puppet shows and decorated the windows of the store. The results were amazing. He remembers that he once painted a nine-foot gorilla in the window for Anthony Browne's book, *Gorilla*. He says those experiences were a great influence on his work. "I'm always thinking, even though it's obviously not ten feet tall, what will make the boldest, cleanest, clearest image."

BECOMING A FULL-TIME AUTHOR AND ILLUSTRATOR: The success of *The Houdini Box* allowed Selznick to become a full-time author/illustrator. Over the past 15 years, he has written and illustrated his own books, and created art for other authors, too.

ILLUSTRATING FOR OTHER AUTHORS: Selznick has illustrated some of the best-loved books of some of the

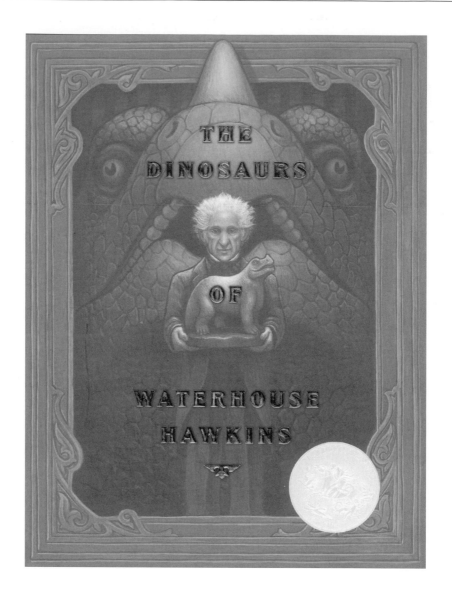

best children's authors. He illustrated Andrew Clements's beloved *Frindle*. He also illustrated *The Doll People* by Ann M. Martin and Laura Godwin.

THE DINOSAURS OF WATERHOUSE HAWKINS: Another favorite book featuring his illustrations is *The Dinosaurs of Waterhouse Hawkins* by Barbara Kerley.

It's about an Englishman who built life-size dinosaurs in the 19th century, before people knew what they really looked like. The book won Selznick a Caldecott Honor in 2001.

WHEN MARIAN SANG: Selznick has illustrated several biographies, too, including one of Marian Anderson. It's called *When Marian Sang,* and was written by Pam Munoz Ryan. (You can read a profile of Marian Anderson in this issue of *Biography for Beginners.*) Selznick's illustrations enrich readers' understanding of the beauty and glory of Anderson's wonderful voice, and of her courageous actions on behalf of equal rights for African-Americans.

HOW HE ILLUSTRATES: In an interview with students, Selznick described how he illustrates a book. "First I read the story, then I go back and underline all the parts where something important is described, like clothing, or hair color, or the furniture in a room. Then I do many quick sketches that are very small (called thumbnail sketches) to get my ideas down.

"I eventually do lots of research and add that to the drawings, and I often photograph models to help me make the drawings more realistic. I think about how the pages should be divided, and what pictures should be used to illustrate those pages. I try many different compositions (ways of arranging the things in the picture). Sometimes I have to start from scratch because the idea isn't working."

Selznick loves the process of working with authors, and also being both author and illustrator. He combined his talents in both areas in *The Boy of a Thousand Faces*. That book also featured his love of monster movies. Selznick's next work was *The Invention of Hugo Cabret*, a book that astonished and delighted readers of all ages.

THE INVENTION OF HUGO CABRET: Selznick calls the book "A Novel in Words and Pictures." But it is truly more than that. The early pages draw a reader from the sky above Paris into the mysterious world of Hugo, who

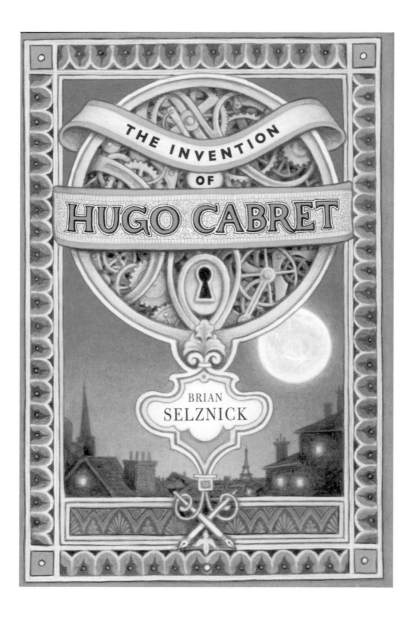

lives in the walls of a train station. The book is many things. It's the story of Hugo, who tries to bring to life an automaton, a clock-like mechanical creature. It's also a recreation of the life of Georges Melies, one of the first filmmakers. In fact, there are several stills from Melies's movies in the book.

The Invention of Hugo Cabret is long—534 pages. But those pages of pencil drawings and text fly by as the reader is taken on an awe-inspiring journey of discovery. Selznick explains that the book started out with just one illustration per chapter. But that wasn't enough for him. He reworked the book, finishing with 284 drawings. "Anything that was just description I replaced with a drawing," he recalls. The illustrations often look like storyboards— the series of stills that filmmakers use to plan movies.

WINNING THE CALDECOTT: *Hugo* became a national bestseller, and in January 2008 won the Caldecott Medal. That is the highest honor in children's book illustration. Selznick was overwhelmed. "It was incredible," he said. "I was exhilarated, delirious."

Selznick was very gracious about sharing the praise the book has received. "I have this award today because of an incredible group of people I've been lucky enough to work with."

FUTURE PLANS: Selznick is now finishing up another in the Doll people series, by Ann Martin and Laura Godwin. Then he's on to another book that he'll both write and illustrate. "I have a couple of ideas for it," he says. "It will again involve the interplay of text and pictures, but it won't be about the cinema."

BRIAN SELZNICK'S HOME AND FAMILY: Selznick has two homes, one in Brooklyn, New York, and one in San

Diego, California. He works in a studio out of his home. He says he has a "whole closet filled with art supplies." He hangs his pictures on a cork wall in front of his desk, "so I can see them all together."

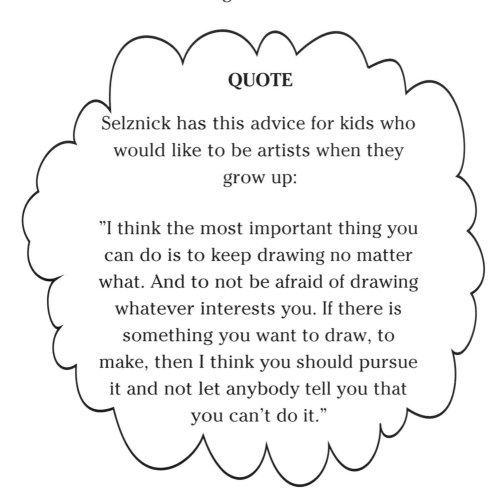

QUOTE

Selznick has this advice for kids who would like to be artists when they grow up:

"I think the most important thing you can do is to keep drawing no matter what. And to not be afraid of drawing whatever interests you. If there is something you want to draw, to make, then I think you should pursue it and not let anybody tell you that you can't do it."

SOME OF BRIAN SELZNICK'S BOOKS:

As Author and Illustrator
The Houdini Box
The Boy of a Thousand Faces
The Invention of Hugo Cabret

As Illustrator

Frindle

The Doll People

The Dinosaurs of Waterhouse Hawkins

Amelia and Eleanor Go for a Ride

When Marian Sang

FOR MORE INFORMATION ABOUT BRIAN SELZNICK:

Write: Scholastic Press
557 Broadway
New York, NY 10012

WORLD WIDE WEB SITES:

http://www.booksense.com/people/archive/selznick.jsp

http://www.cbcbooks.org/cbcmagazine/meet/brian_
selznick.html

http://www.theinventionofhugocabret.com/

http://www.gritskids.com/Interviews/ill_selznick.html

http://scholastic.com

Name Index

Listed below are the names of all individuals who have appeared in *Biography for Beginners*, followed by the issue and year in which they appear.

Adu, Freddy, Spring 2005

Aguilera, Christina, Spring 2001

Aliki, Spring '96

Allen, Tim, Fall '96

Anderson, Marian, Spring 2008

Angelou, Maya, Fall 2006

Annan, Kofi, Fall 2000

Applegate, K.A., Spring 2000

Armstrong, Lance, Fall 2002

Avi, Spring 2003

Babbitt, Natalie, Spring 2006

Ballard, Robert, Fall 2002

Barber, Ronde, Spring 2004

Barber, Tiki, Spring 2004

Bearden, Romare, Spring 2008

Bemelmans, Ludwig, Spring 2004

Bentley, Wilson "Snowflake," Spring 2003

Berenstain, Jan, Fall '95

Berenstain, Stan, Fall '95

Berners-Lee, Tim, Fall 2007

Blair, Bonnie, Spring '95

Blume, Judy, Fall '95

Bonds, Barry, Fall 2002

Brady, Tom, Fall 2004

Brandy, Fall '96

Brett, Jan, Spring '95

Bridwell, Norman, Fall '99

Brown, Marc, Spring '98

Brown, Margaret Wise, Spring 2006

Brunhoff, Jean de, Spring 2007

Bryan, Zachery Ty, Spring '97

Bryant, Kobe, Fall '99

Bunting, Eve, Fall 2001

Burton, LeVar, Spring '98

Burton, Virginia Lee, Spring '97

Bush, George W., Fall 2001

Bush, Laura, Spring 2002

Butcher, Susan, Fall 2000

Byars, Betsy, Fall 2002

Bynes, Amanda, Spring 2005

Cannon, Janell, Spring '99

Cannon, Nick, Spring 2003

Subject Index

This index includes subjects, occupations, and ethnic and minority origins for individuals who have appeared in *Biography for Beginners.*

artists
Bearden, Romare, Spring 2008
GrandPré, Mary, Fall 2003
Lin, Maya, Spring 2001
Lobel, Anita, Spring 2008
Nechita, Alexandra, Spring 2000
Pinkney, Jerry, Spring 2002
Rohmann, Eric, Spring 2004
Sabuda, Robert, Spring 2005

Asian-Americans
Kwan, Michelle, Spring 2002
Lin, Maya, Spring 2001
Wie, Michelle, Spring 2004
Yamaguchi, Kristi, Fall '97

astronauts
Jemison, Mae, Fall '96
Lucid, Shannon, Fall '97
Ochoa, Ellen, Spring 2005

athletes
Adu, Freddy, Spring 2005
Armstrong, Lance, Fall 2002
Barber, Ronde, Spring 2004
Barber, Tiki, Spring 2004
Blair, Bonnie, Spring '95
Bonds, Barry, Fall 2002

Brady, Tom, Fall 2004
Bryant, Kobe, Fall '99
Butcher, Susan, Fall 2000
Carter, Vince, Fall 2001
Duncan, Tim, Fall 2005
Gordon, Jeff, Spring 2000
Gretzky, Wayne, Spring '96
Griffey, Ken Jr., Fall, '95
Hamm, Mia, Spring '98
Hawk, Tony, Fall 2001
Hill, Grant, Fall '97
James, LeBron, Fall 2007
Jeter, Derek, Fall 2000
Jones, Marion, Spring 2001
Jordan, Michael, Spring '97
Joyner-Kersee, Jackie, Fall '95
Kerrigan, Nancy, Fall '95
Kwan, Michelle, Spring 2002
Leslie, Lisa, Fall 2006
Lipinski, Tara, Spring '98
Manning, Eli, Spring 2008
Martinez, Pedro, Spring 2001
McGwire, Mark, Spring '99
Miller, Shannon, Spring '95
Moceanu, Dominique, Fall '98
Montana, Joe, Spring '95
Olajuwon, Hakeem, Spring '96

autobiographer

baseball players

Carter, Vince, Fall 2001

Hamm, Mia, Spring '98

Hill, Grant, Fall '97

Jones, Marion, Spring 2001

Jordan, Michael, Spring '97

Joyner-Kersee, Jackie, Fall '95

Kerrigan, Nancy, Fall '95

Kwan, Michelle, Spring 2002

Leslie, Lisa, Fall 2006

Lipinski, Tara, Spring '98

Miller, Shannon, Spring'95

Moceanu, Dominique, Fall '98

Phelps, Michael, Spring 2006

Robinson, David, Fall '96

Scurry, Briana, Fall '99

Strug, Kerri, Spring '97

Swoopes, Sheryl, Spring 2000

Van Dyken, Amy, Spring 2000

Williams, Serena, Fall 2003

Yamaguchi, Kristi, Fall '97

paper engineer

Sabuda, Robert, Spring 2005

photographer

Bentley, Wilson "Snowflake," Spring 2003

Parks, Gordon, Spring 2007

physicist

Berners-Lee, Tim, Fall 2007

Hawking, Stephen, Fall 2007

Kamen, Dean, Spring 2006

poets

Angelou, Maya, Fall 2006

Prelutsky, Jack, Spring '97

Silverstein, Shel, Spring '97

Willard, Nancy, Spring 2004

Yolen, Jane, Spring '99

politicians

Bush, George W., Fall 2001

Cheney, Dick, Fall 2003

Clinton, Bill, Spring '95

Gore, Al, Fall '97

Mandela, Nelson, Spring '95

President of South Africa

Mandela, Nelson, Spring '95

Presidents of the United States

Bush, George W., Fall 2001

Clinton, Bill, Spring '95

Birthday Index

January

3 Eli Manning (1981)
7 Katie Couric (1957)
8 Stephen Hawking (1942)
12 John Lasseter (1957)
14 Shannon Lucid (1943)
17 Shari Lewis (1934)
21 Hakeem Olajuwon (1963)
26 Vince Carter (1977)
28 Wayne Gretzky (1961)
29 Bill Peet (1915)
Rosemary Wells (1943)
Oprah Winfrey (1954)
30 Dick Cheney (1941)
31 Bryan Collier (1967)

February

2 Judith Viorst (1931)
4 Rosa Parks (1913)
5 David Wiesner (1956)
7 Laura Ingalls Wilder (1867)
9 Wilson "Snowflake" Bentley (1865)
11 Jane Yolen (1939)
Brandy (1979)
12 Judy Blume (1938)
David Small (1945)
13 Mary GrandPré (1954)
15 Norman Bridwell (1928)
Amy Van Dyken (1973)
16 LeVar Burton (1957)
17 Michael Jordan (1963)
Marian Anderson (1897)
22 Steve Irwin (1962)
24 Steven Jobs (1955)
27 Chelsea Clinton (1980)

March

2 Leo Dillon (1933)
Dr. Seuss (1904)
David Satcher (1941)
3 Patricia MacLachlan (1938)
Jackie Joyner-Kersee (1962)
4 Garrett Morgan (1877)
Dav Pilkey (1966)
5 Mem Fox (1946)

Jake Lloyd (1989)

6 Chris Raschka (1959)

8 Robert Sabuda (1965)

10 Shannon Miller (1977)

11 Ezra Jack Keats (1916)
Virginia Hamilton (1936)
Diane Dillon (1933)

15 Ruth Bader Ginsburg (1933)

16 Shaquille O'Neal (1972)

17 Mia Hamm (1972)

18 Bonnie Blair (1964)

20 Fred Rogers (1928)
Lois Lowry (1937)
Louis Sachar (1954)

21 Rosie O'Donnell (1962)

25 DiCamillo, Kate (1964)
Sheryl Swoopes (1971)
Danica Patrick (1982)

31 Al Gore (1948)

April

3 Jane Goodall (1934)
Amanda Bynes (1986)

4 Maya Angelou (1928)

5 Richard Peck (1934)
Colin Powell (1937)
Dean Kamen (1951)

7 RondeBarber (1975)
Tiki Barber (1975)

8 Kofi Annan (1938)

12 Beverly Cleary (1916)
Tony Hawk (1968)

15 Tim Duncan (1976)
Emma Watson (1990)

16 Garth Williams (1912)

18 Melissa Joan Hart (1976)

26 Patricia Reilly Giff (1935)

27 Ludwig Bemelmans (1898)
Coretta Scott King (1927)
Barbara Park (1947)

May

4 Don Wood (1945)

6 Judy Delton (1931)
Ted Lewin (1935)

10 Leo Lionni (1910)
Christopher Paul Curtis (1953)
Ellen Ochoa (1958)

11 Peter Sis (1949)

12 Betsy Lewin (1937)

14 George Lucas (1944)
Emmitt Smith (1969)

16 Margret Rey (1906)

17 Gary Paulsen (1939)

20 Mary Pope Osborne (1949)

22 Arnold Lobel (1933)

23 Margaret Wise Brown (1910)

29 Andrew Clements (1949)

June

2 Freddy Adu (1989)

2 Anita Lobel (1934)

5 Richard Scarry (1919)

6 Cynthia Rylant (1954)
Larisa Oleynik (1981)
Tim Berners-Lee (1955)

9 Freddie Highmore (1992)

10 Maurice Sendak (1928)
Tara Lipinski (1982)

11 Joe Montana (1956)

13 Tim Allen (1953)

15 Jack Horner (1946)

18 Chris Van Allsburg (1949)

25 Eric Carle (1929)

23 Wilma Rudolph (1940)

26 Nancy Willard (1936)
Derek Jeter (1974)
Michael Vick (1980)

30 Robert Ballard (1971)
Michael Phelps (1985)

July

2 Dave Thomas (1932)

6 George W. Bush (1946)

7 Lisa Leslie (1972)
Michelle Kwan (1980)

11 E.B. White (1899)
Patricia Polacco (1944)

12 Kristi Yamaguchi (1972)

13 Stephanie Kwolek (1923)

14 Peggy Parish (1927)

14 Laura Numeroff (1953)

18 Nelson Mandela (1918)

24 Barry Bonds (1964)
Mara Wilson (1987)

26 Jan Berenstain (1923)

28 Beatrix Potter (1866)
Natalie Babbitt (1932)
Jim Davis (1945)

31 J.K. Rowling (1965)
Daniel Radcliffe (1989)

August

2 Betsy Byars (1928)

3 Tom Brady (1977)

4 Jeff Gordon (1971)

6 Barbara Cooney (1917)
David Robinson (1965)

9 Patricia McKissack (1944)
Whitney Houston (1963)

11 Joanna Cole (1944)

12 Walter Dean Myers (1937)

Fredrick McKissack (1939)

Ann M. Martin (1955)

15 Linda Ellerbee (1944)

16 Matt Christopher (1917)

18 Paula Danziger (1944)

19 Bill Clinton (1946)

21 Stephen Hillenburg (1961)

23 Kobe Bryant (1978)

24 Cal Ripken Jr. (1960)

26 Mother Teresa (1910)

27 Alexandra Nechita (1985)

28 Brian Pinkney (1961)

29 Temple Grandin (1947)

30 Virginia Lee Burton (1909)

Sylvia Earle (1935)

Donald Crews (1938)

31 Itzhak Perlman (1945)

September

1 Gloria Estefan (1958)

2 Bearden Romare (1911)

3 Aliki (1929)

7 Briana Scurry (1971)

8 Jack Prelutsky (1940)

Jon Scieszka (1954)

Jonathan Taylor Thomas (1982)

15 McCloskey, Robert (1914)

Tomie dePaola (1934)

16 H. A. Rey (1898)

Roald Dahl (1916)

17 Kevin Clash (1960)

18 Ben Carson (1951)

Lance Armstrong (1971)

24 Jim Henson (1936)

25 Andrea Davis Pinkney (1963)

25 Will Smith (1968)

26 Serena Williams (1981)

28 Hilary Duff (1987)

29 Stan Berenstain (1923)

30 Dominique Moceanu (1981)

October

1 Mark McGwire (1963)

5 Grant Hill (1972)

Maya Lin (1959)

6 Lonnie Johnson (1949)

7 Yo-Yo Ma (1955)

8 Faith Ringgold (1930)

9 Zachery Ty Bryan (1981)

10 James Marshall (1942)

11 Michelle Wie (1989)

12 Marion Jones (1975)

13 Nancy Kerrigan (1969)

17 Mae Jemison (1954)
Nick Cannon (1980)
18 Wynton Marsalis (1961)
Zac Efron (1987)
22 Ichiro Suzuki (1973)
23 Pele (1940)
25 Pedro Martinez (1971)
26 Hillary Clinton (1947)
26 Steven Kellogg (1941)
Eric Rohmann (1957)
28 Bill Gates (1955)
31 Katherine Paterson (1932)

November

3 Janell Cannon (1957)
4 Laura Bush (1946)
9 Lois Ehlert (1934)
12 Sammy Sosa (1968)
14 Astrid Lindgren (1907)
William Steig (1907)
Condoleezza Rice (1954)
15 Daniel Pinkwater (1941)
19 Savion Glover (1973)
Kerri Strug (1977)
Ken Griffey Jr. (1969)

23 Miley Cyrus (1992)
25 Marc Brown (1946)
26 Charles Schulz (1922)
27 Bill Nye (1955)
Kevin Henkes (1960)
Jaleel White (1977)
29 C.S. Lewis (1898)
30 Gordon Parks (1912)

December

1 Jan Brett (1949)
5 Frankie Muniz (1985)
9 Jean de Brunhoff (1899)
10 Raven (1985)
18 Christina Aguilera (1980)
14 Vanessa Anne Hudgens (1988)
19 Eve Bunting (1928)
22 Jerry Pinkney (1939)
23 Avi (1937)
26 Susan Butcher (1954)
30 LeBron James (1984)
Mercer Mayer (1943)
Tiger Woods (1975)